I0463595

# Your Fired: Rebuilding Your Professional Life

## After Getting Fired, Laid Off, Demoted, or Down-Sized

By Paul Oder

Minute Help Press

© 2010. All Rights Reserved

# Table of Contents:

# Introduction

Have you recently lost your job? Were you fired? It isn't the end of the world. The economy might be tough right now, but jobs are out there and people are hiring. If you have recently been fired stop stressing and start making a plan. After all, you won't find your perfect new job if you don't get out and start looking for it.

Many people view getting fired as the closing of a door, when in reality it is the start of a new opportunity. While you won't be working in your old job anymore, you now have the opportunity to reinvent yourself. You can try new things, go new places or find a position better suited to your needs. Getting fired might be the wakeup call that you need to get out and try something different. It is an opportunity in disguise.

After getting fired it is common to feel frustrated, discouraged and scared. Many people worry that they won't be able to find a new job or pay their monthly bills. While these are valid concerns, they shouldn't be at the top of your mind. Instead, you should think about what you are going to do now. How are you going to start over and find a new job? What new opportunities await you? Don't live in the past and think about what could have been. Accept what has happened and move on.

Finding a new job will take time, and the sooner you start looking the sooner you will start working again. Get out of bed, put on your thinking cap and start planning your new future today. Don't let getting fired ruin your life. You are in control and it is up to you to make something great out of an unpleasant situation.

# Now What?!

Many people are in a state of shock after they find out that they have been fired or laid off. If this is your first time going through this situation, you might not know where to go or even what to do next. You might be wondering things like, "How am I going to pay my bills?" or, "What next?"

## Take a Look at Your Finances

Financial matters are important, so one of the first things that you need to do after getting fired is take a look at your finances. What are your expenses each month? Do you have any other sources of income? How much do you have in savings? What can you cut back?

# Apply for Unemployment

It is also important to apply for unemployment as quickly as possible. Sometimes it can take several weeks to process paperwork. Filing quickly is essential for getting financial help as quickly as possible. Contact your state's unemployment office and fill out an application. Many states will let you apply online, which speeds up the process and saves you a trip down to the unemployment office.

When you file your paperwork you will need to have quite a bit of information available. The exact information needed will vary by state, but in general you will need to provide your name, address, phone number, social security number, information about your previous employer (including name, address and phone number), dates of employment and salary information. A lot the information you need will be found on an old paystub, so have one with you when you apply.

You should know that there are rules governing who can apply for unemployment. If you quit your last job or were fired with cause, there may be difficulty in getting unemployment. You should still fill out the paperwork though. If your claim is denied, you can always file an appeal.

# Taking Care of Financial Matters

Once you figure out your expenses and if you will qualify for unemployment, you can start making decisions about your finances. These decisions can be difficult, but don't avoid them. The sooner you face your finances, the more options that you will have available. Many people have a hard time paying their bills after they lose their job.

# Mortgage

If you know that you are going to be unable to pay your mortgage after losing your job it is best to act as quickly as possible. This will help you to avoid foreclosure.

If you have built up equity in your home, you can consider refinancing your home loan and using the cash to pay your mortgage. This will only work for those that have a significant amount of value built up in their home and good credit. Another option is to put your home up for sale. In some cases your lender might be willing to accept a short sale if you cannot sell your home for the full amount that you owe.

Some homeowners talk with their lender about forbearance. A forbearance is often granted in times of temporary financial hardship. Basically your loan payments will be suspended for a period of time. Once the payment schedule resumes you will pay your monthly payment plus repayment toward the suspended payments. While this is not a long term option, it can help you to keep your home. Typically forbearances are very short term, 6 months or less. Talk to your lender for more details and to see if this applies to you.

# Credit Cards

Credit cards are another difficult situation for those that don't have a job and a paycheck. It can be tempting to use your credit cards to pay other bills. This should be avoided whenever possible. This will only get you deeper in debt and will create more problems. First and foremost, contact your creditors and explain your situation. If you won't be able to make your monthly payments, ask that they be lowered or that you be given an extension. Remember, creditors don't want you to file bankruptcy and if you are honest about what you can do, they will often work with you. This can help you to get back on your feet financially.

# What Are My Options?

## Consider Working as a Consultant

If you have specific skills you may be able to earn a little cash as you search for jobs by working as a freelance consultant. This can be a great way to keep your skills up to date while you search for new jobs. Plus it can bring in a little extra cash. If you file for unemployment the money earned may be taken from your unemployment check, so make sure that you find out what restrictions apply before getting started. It is also important to make sure that you adhere to local laws regarding licensing and taxes.

# Start Over or Start Again

 Once you have reviewed your finances and have your bills under control, you can start planning out the rest of your life. You know that you need to get a new job, but you will have to decide what you want to do, where you want to live and how you are going to achieve these goals. Losing your job gives you the opportunity to make a fresh start. If you want to enter a new field or to try something new, now is the perfect time.

# Explore Your Options

You have an opportunity right now to make a change if you want to. You just need to decide if you want to try something new or find a new job in the same field.

Sit down and make a list of everything that you want to or know how to do. If you have dreamed of heading back to school to become a nurse or if you have been thinking about finally getting your contractor's license, write it down on your list of possibilities. As you come up with ideas think about the pros and the cons to each.

# Pros of Staying in the Same Field

If you choose to get another job in the same type of industry and position there are some major benefits. You already know what to expect from this type of position. This means that it will be very easy to determine what kind of salary you need and what the working conditions will be like.

If you have a lot of experience it might be easier for you to land a position in the industry that you are already in. Employers will know that you will need very little training and that you will come to their company ready to jump in and get to work. Your experience will make you a valuable part of any new team and you will be able to offer input and advice from day one.

# Cons of Staying in the Same Field

While staying in the same field might be the easiest choice, it isn't without a few downsides. Make sure that you consider the cons as well as the pros before making your final choice. You have a rare opportunity to try something new, so make sure that you consider all of your possibilities and that you don't simply choose the easiest option.

One major con to staying in the same field is that you might lose your job again. Ask yourself why you lost your current job. Were you fired or laid off? Is the industry experiencing a downturn? If you are working in a field that isn't growing you might find a new job only to find that you will lose it again soon. Or you may have trouble finding work since many others are probably looking as well. Think about your industry and the employment prospects both now and in the future to determine if your current industry is a good one to stay in.

Another con is that you will be doing the same thing again. If you were bored or tired of your last position, don't assume that things will automatically be different in a new position. If you remain in the same industry you will likely have a similar situation to the one you just left. If you were unhappy in your last job, you might want to consider switching to a new career where you will be happier.

# Should I Return to School?

## Pros of Going Back to School/ Learning a New Trade

Going back to school or learning a new trade will open new career opportunities to you. You can learn a new trade or gain the education needed to enter a new field. You can also learn new skills that will make you more employable in your current field. This can help you to find better positions and higher pay as you search for a new job.

The job market is tough right now and it is important to really distinguish yourself from other candidates if you want to stand out. Getting more education can do this. It will also make more positions a possibility.

When you lose your job you have a rare opportunity to reinvent yourself. You can become anything you want and start a new life and a new career. If you have been wanting to go back to school, now is the perfect time.

# Cons of Going Back to School

While getting an education will provide many opportunities, it is not without cost. In addition to the actual expense of school you will have to devote your time and your energy into learning new skills. There are other cons associated with going back to school as well.

When you are in school you might not be able to work as much as you can when you aren't taking classes. If you don't have money coming in it can be difficult to pay your bills and keep afloat. Of course, if you are receiving unemployment benefits, this can help pay your bills while you are in school or a training program.

Starting in a new industry can also be difficult. While you will obtain an education you will have no applicable experience when you get done. This might mean starting over at the bottom of the corporate ladder. Your salary will likely start off lower and you will have to work your way up once again.

Finally there is the financial expense. Going to school can be very expensive. There is the cost of books, tuition, supplies and more. Since you are out of work it might seem almost impossible to pay for formal education or trade school.

# Financial Aid

One of the biggest reasons that people don't get training or education is the cost. These courses can be expensive and take a lot of time. However, getting training can help you to qualify for new positions, to find more stable career options and to increase your earning potential. Training and education isn't the right choice in every situation, but if you want to increase your marketability, don't discount education simply because you can't afford it. There are other ways to pay for school or training programs.

Financial aid is a great way to help finance an education. Many people assume that financial aid is only available to those going to a college or a university, but this is not true. There are financial aid opportunities in many career fields. Whether you are interested in cosmetology, bookkeeping, automotive repair or some other field, there are opportunities available for you.

# Federal Financial Aid

One of the easiest ways to get money for school is from the federal government. To apply for federal student aid you will first need to fill out a special form known as the FAFSA. This stands for Free Application for Federal Student Aid. As the name implies, this application is free. There is no risk in seeing if you qualify for funding and how much you can get.

Your school will be able to help you with your FAFSA application if you have any questions. Filling it out is pretty simple and almost everyone qualifies. You will need some information to fill out this form so gather up your last tax return, your social security number and school information before starting the form. When you are ready, you can find and fill out the FAFSA online.

Once you complete your FAFSA, your school will be able to tell you what kind of aid you qualify for. There are a few options that may be available to you. Generally you will receive grants, subsidized loans and unsubsidized loans or a combination of any of the three. Grants are basically a free gift and won't have to be paid back as long as you meet specific qualifications. Subsidized loans will have to be repaid, but while you are in school the government will pay your interest which can save a lot of money. Unsubsidized loans will have to be repaid with interest, but are a very affordable way to finance an education and you won't have to make any payments until you have been out of school for at least 6 months.

## Scholarships

Most people automatically assume that scholarships are for high school students and recent graduates. While there might be some opportunities that are only available to this age group, you can find plenty of opportunities no matter your age or educational background. When looking for scholarships focus on your intended course of study and any organizations that you belong to. You may be able to find funding for your education this way.

As you find private scholarships make sure that you follow the application instructions closely. There are typically various deadlines that must be followed as well as strict application guidelines. Some require you to fill out an application while others ask for a resume. In addition some scholarships will require you to write essays or get letters of recommendation. Scholarships can make an education a possibility, but you won't receive any if you don't follow the guidelines for applying.

## Tax Credits

There are also a variety of different tax credits that can make school more affordable. Talk with your tax preparer and find out how much of your education related expenses you can write off. In many cases you can write off most of your educational expenses including interest paid on student loans and tuition. If you decide to go back to school and learn new skills, make sure that you take advantage of the tax breaks that are afforded to you.

# College or Trade School?

If you have decided to head back to school, the question is now- what kind of school? There are many great educational options and they will vary quite a bit depending on the path that you are looking to pursue. In some cases a two or four year degree will be the best choice, but in other situations you might find that professional training courses or trade school better fit the bill.

As you think about your educational options you will have to consider your career goals. For example if you want to become an engineer, enrolling in cosmetology school won't help you to enter your chosen career field. On the other hand if you want to do hair or nails, cosmetology school is the ideal choice. Think about where you want to end up career wise and find out what kind of education is needed.

# Two Year/ Four Year Colleges

If you are considering careers that require a minimum of an Associates or Bachelors degree, you will need to enroll in a two year or four year college. If you have a college education already you may be able to take classes in your new field and get a second degree relatively quickly. Past college credit will also apply toward your courses.

Make sure that you talk with an admissions counselor right away. They will be able to help you to see how past courses will apply to your current program and will tell you which classes you need to take. Don't try to figure out your course schedule on your own. This can result in taking the wrong classes and having to spend extra time and money on school. An admissions counselor will help you chart the most effective course for efficient completion.

Some colleges also offer certificate programs that can help you to get started in various careers. Check with your local college and find out if there are any special certificate programs available if you are interested in this option. This can often be cheaper than learning similar skills at a trade school.

As you consider which schools to enroll in remember that private colleges are often much more expensive than public schools. Many people choose to go with the convenience of a private school without realizing that public schools offer similar programs. Many public colleges offer online degrees, night schedules and other flexible options which can help you to get an education while looking for jobs or attending to other obligations.

# Professional or Trade Schools

Trade schools are another great way to start a new career or learn new skills. Trade schools can provide you with the hands-on learning that you need to enter a variety of different fields. Whether you are interested in automotive repair, computers and technology or floral design, you will be able to find a trade school to teach you the skills that you need.

Trade schools generally offer a much quicker path to returning to the workforce than two year or four year colleges. Time required will vary based on the program that you select. Research your desired profession to find out what the educational requirements are.

# Which Should You Choose?

The decision between a college and a trade school will come down to personal preference and the career that you are looking to pursue. Decide what you want to accomplish first and then go about making a plan to make it happen. Don't just enroll in school because you don't know what else to do. Make a plan first and decide where you want your career to go. This will ensure that you use your time wisely and that you get an education that can translate into a career.

# Words of Advice

Whether you choose to start over or start again, this time between jobs should be a time of reflection. Analyze what went wrong in your last position and create a plan to keep it from happening again. Decide where you want your future to go and then make plans to get yourself there. Don't be discouraged. This will require motivation and determination. Consider this new beginning an opportunity and take full advantage of it.

# How to Find a Job

Now it is time to start finding a new job. This is intimidating to many people that have just been fired, but there is no need to worry. You have many great skills that will be a value to any employer. Remember your value and don't get discouraged if the job hunt takes a little longer than you were hoping. Finding a job that is a perfect match for your skills and personality will take time.

Finding a job will require using several different techniques. Don't limit yourself to just one strategy. Try several. This way you will reach more employers and will hear about more potential job openings. Persistence is critical, even when you feel discouraged.

## Network

If you want to hear about the newest jobs and have a connection with various companies, networking is critical. As soon as you lose your job, start talking. Let friends and family know what you are looking for. They may have a connection that could result in a job lead for you.

In addition to talking with friends and family it is also a good idea to contact old co-workers and associates. Try to talk to people that have a connection in the industry you are interested in. Explain your position and what you can offer and ask for help. While it might feel uncomfortable to ask others if they know anyone that can help you get a job, it is one of the most effective job hunting methods around.

## Online Searching

The Internet is filled with resources for job hunters. Make sure that you devote a little time each day to searching online job boards. These are filled with current positions in a variety of different industries and can help you find a great job.

When using online job boards you will be facing a lot of competition. Make sure that you put your best face forward in each and every application. Don't rush through an application or send in a resume that you haven't spent time on. Take the same level of care when applying online as when using other methods of finding work.

Generally it is a good idea to create an account at several online job sites like Monster, HotJobs and Indeed. If you are looking in a specific industry you should also search for specific job hunting sites within your career field. For example those working in the journalism industry might try JournalismJobs.com and those looking for government jobs should try USAJobs.gov.

Since these jobs boards get a lot of responses from companies you need to stay on top of them. Try to get applications in quickly, two to three days from the initial posting if possible. Remember that if the perfect candidate comes along before you apply, your resume won't even be considered, even if you are qualified. Check these sites daily and quickly apply for positions once you find those that you are interested in.

Don't waste your time applying for jobs that you aren't interested in or that you aren't qualified for. There are many jobs out there are you will make better use of your time finding positions that you are well-suited for than applying to everything. Take your time and always follow all of the instructions in the job posting.

# Talk with Recruiters

Recruiters can be a great resource when finding a job, however they can be a little tricky to find. Basically recruiters are hired by companies to go out and find qualified candidates. If you impress a recruiter, they will then sell you to the company. This makes your job a lot easier.

Recruiters can be found in a variety of different places. Many times you will encounter recruiters as you search for jobs. They are often responsible for posting jobs on online job boards. You might also run into recruiters at a job fair.

When working with recruiters always behave in the same manner that you would when working directly with the company. Some recruiters are actual employees of the hiring company and others are just contractors that are working on a commission basis for the company.

# Job Fairs

Many companies send recruiters to job fairs to find potential candidates. When you go to job fairs take along several generic resumes. It is best to use a very generic resume for job fairs since you don't know what types of positions you will be encountering. Talk with everyone at the job fair. If nothing else it is a great opportunity to network. However, in many cases you will find job leads as well.

When talking with recruiters act as though you are in an informal interview. Stay on topic and sell yourself to the recruiter while asking questions about the positions. Always maintain a professional demeanor at job fairs.

# Check Out the Classifieds

If you want a local job your newspaper's classifieds might be your best bet. Often you will find a different assortment of jobs here than you will online. Since only a local market is exposed to these ads you will generally encounter less competition. A downside to using classifieds is that they generally provide very little information about the position or the company, which can make it difficult to create an applicable resume.

# Social Networking

If you haven't started using social networking in your job search then you are missing out on a new opportunity. This is a great way to reconnect with old friends, coworkers and associates and can be very useful in finding a new job.

Send a personal message to those that you think might be able to help you in your job hunt. Make sure that your profile is professional. Future employers won't be impressed if you rant about how much you hated your last job or if you spend all hours of the day playing social networking games. Make sure that your profile represents the image that you want others to see.

It is also a good idea to check your social networking privacy settings before your start sending out your resume. Some companies will look up potential candidates and if there is anything that you don't want them to see, you had better adjust your privacy settings.

# Searching Locally

If you have big companies or government offices nearby you might be able to find job boards and positions that aren't listed in other places. Stop by and check these often for new positions.

# Choosing How to Best Spend Your Time

While there are many ways to search for jobs, you only have so much time in the day. As a job hunter it is important to be organized and to carefully prioritize the many tasks that you need to complete. It is a good idea to create a daily schedule and to block out specific amounts of time for each important activity. Try to fill your days with a variety of different tasks so that you aren't relying entirely on one job hunting method.

Remember that some tasks are more productive than others. For example, if you have the opportunity to go to a job fair take advantage of it. You will meet more people and make more connections than you will by spending a similar amount of time on the Internet.

Some Internet searching methods are more productive than others as well. Try to use searching methods that will lead you to jobs with less exposure. For example, if you search on Craigslist for openings you might encounter less competition than when applying for jobs on Monster.

# Which Jobs Should You Apply For?

There are many positions out there and it will be impossible to apply for them all. How will you decide which positions are worth your time and which to avoid? Here are some tips for finding the perfect job.

Find Jobs That You Qualify For- This doesn't mean that you can't apply for jobs where your skills are a stretch for meeting minimum qualifications, but generally means avoiding positions where you aren't qualified at all. For example, if you have years of food service experience you might not want to spend your time applying for a position as a hospital administrator.

Determine Your Requirements- When job hunting it is easy to get desperate and to take the first position that comes around. This will leave you unhappy and will probably result in your rejoining the job hunt quickly. Create a list of your minimum needs. If you don't want to commute more than 30 miles or if you need to work nights, make sure that you write these requirements down. If you have a few basic requirements you can determine which positions will work for you.

Choose Recent Openings- Jobs often fill quickly, so don't waste your time filling out applications for positions that have been open for several months. These positions are probably filled. If you do find an older position that you are especially qualified for you can always send a letter to the company explaining your qualifications and offering your services if the position is still open.

Remember What You Want- Don't settle for positions that aren't what you are looking for. Keep your career goals in mind and find a new job that is an upgrade from what you had before. Even though you have been fired you deserve to be happy at work.

## Beware of Scams

As you search for jobs you will almost certainly encounter a scam or two. These scams aim to prey on the desperation of job seekers. Often they seek to get money or to lead job seekers astray. Here are some guidelines for recognizing and avoiding common employment scams.

If It Seems to Good To Be True- It Probably Is. Would you pay someone $30 per hour to stuff envelopes? Of course not. No employer in their right mind is going to either. If a job offers high pay for minimal work, don't waste your time applying.

Don't Pay For Employment Opportunities. Many people say that they will offer you a great business opportunity if you pay them or that they will help you find a great job for a fee. These offers are generally scams. If you are considering paying for employment services always check the company out with the Better Business Bureau first. Don't pay for access to secret job banks. The only employment services that you should ever consider paying for are resume writing or distribution and other similar services. Reputable companies don't charge people to apply.

Don't Pay a Recruiter. Recruiters generally earn a living by connecting employees with employers. They receive a commission from companies for each hire that they instigate. Don't pay a recruiter for their services since this is more than likely a scam.

Federal Job Scams.  Many employment scams revolve around helping people to find government jobs. You don't need to spend money to apply for jobs with the federal government. Every position is listed on the government's employment website USAJobs.gov.

Don't Give Out Too Much Information. When applying for jobs online you have to be very careful. There may fake job postings looking to steal your personal information. Don't provide employers with personal information like your social security number or bank account information online or over the phone. If this information is needed you can provide it in person at the interview or once you have been hired.

Beware if Your Job Requires Money Transfers. If you are hired to do money transfers or check cashing for companies you should probably assume that the job is a scam. Generally this scam involves having you deposit fraudulent checks in your bank account and to wire money to someone else. These scams will leave you without money once the fraud is discovered.

Always Monitor Your Social Security Number While Job Hunting. While job hunting you are at an increased risk for becoming a victim of identity theft. Protect yourself by monitoring your credit and immediately reporting problems should anything occur.

## Standing Out

The job market is very competitive right now. This can mean that hundreds of people are applying for the same positions that you are. Getting selected might sound impossible, but it is not. In fact if you understand what employers are looking for you can make yourself stand out from the competition. This will result in more invitations to interview and more job offers.

If you were fired from your last job, it is especially important to be very careful when creating your resume. You want to highlight your strengths rather than raising concerns or worries in the mind of the hiring manager.

# What Should I Leave Off of My Resume?

Many people that have been fired worry that it is dishonest or wrong to leave past jobs off of their resume. This is not true. Your resume isn't supposed to tell employers everything about you. It is basically a sales pitch to help employers see how you could be a good choice for their company. Your resume will help you get to the interview where you can have an opportunity to explain any gaps on your resume.

If you were fired from a short term position, under a year, feel free to leave it off of your resume. While this will create gaps, they are generally more forgivable than a firing at least in the eyes of the hiring manager. However, it can be appropriate to include positions where you were fired, especially if you have notable achievements or learned valuable skills. Think about the position and determine if it adds to your resume or detracts from it.

Many people that have been fired feel discouraged or embarrassed. Don't apologize on your resume. Show confidence and explain how you are a value. Getting fired does not mean that you can't help an employer to achieve their goals. In fact you probably learned important lessons from getting fired that you couldn't have learned otherwise. Be confident and show this confidence on your resume.

If you do wish to include positions that you were fired from on your resume, don't mention that you were fired. This will raise red flags over something that might not be an issue. You may have been fired but you can still provide valuable assistance to a new employer. Getting fired might not have been your fault and if it was it may have taught you a valuable lesson.

## What Do Employers Want to See?

Employers want to know what you can do for them. They have a problem and are looking for a solution. It is your job to explain how you can solve their problems. Look at resume as a sales pitch and use it to show future employers what you have to offer. Let them know how you will solve their problems.

# Custom Resumes for Each Position

Employers want to know what you can offer specifically to them. So do your research. Learn about each company that you are applying to and customize your resume to their needs. While this will take a little extra time it is worth the effort. Plus, the research you do will help you during the interview process as well. Create a custom objective for each job and tailor your skills and abilities for the position you are applying for. A resume for a sales position will focus on different skills than a resume for an engineering position.

For example, if you are applying for a position that requires secretarial experience and you have none, you can show how past positions have prepared you for this job by highlighting those aspects. If you answered phones while working as a janitor or if you coordinated company schedules at your last job make sure that you point out these specific skills. Create an objective that shows how you are qualified by saying something like, "I am seeking a secretarial position where I can utilize my skills obtained in many different industries." This will help future employers understand what you have to offer.

# Action Statements

Use action words and statements to create interest in your resume. Rather than saying, "Handled filing and billing," say something like, "Created a new comprehensive filing system that increased company efficiency 15% and handled all company billing to more than 1,000 clients." The second statement stands out and shows results.

# Don't Make Additional Work for the Employer

Employers are looking to hire someone to solve a problem, not to make more work for their hiring managers. Make sure that your resume is easy to read and that it is easy to find the pertinent information. If you are applying for a specific position always include the job posting number so that there is no question about which position you are seeking.

Always include plenty of contact information. Some employers prefer to get additional information via email while others like to call. If you provide all of your contact information they will be able to contact you in the manner that is most convenient for them.

Never ask an employer to contact you to confirm receipt of your resume. It may be appropriate to follow up with an employer, but you should be the one doing this. Don't expect employers to put any extra effort into your resume. They may be reviewing hundreds and it is important that you make their job as easy as possible.

# Resume Help

## Perfect Spelling and Grammar

Your resume needs to show your attention to detail. Make sure that you carefully review your resume for grammar and spelling errors. Proper formatting is also important. Once your resume is completed, read over it several times. It is also a good idea to have someone else review your resume looking for errors.

In addition to proper formatting and grammar it is important to make sure that your entire resume is consistent. If you decide to bold job titles, make sure that each job title is remembered. Use the same font throughout the entire resume. Generally it is best to avoid fancy fonts. Choose something that is easy to read and that looks professional.

Your resume is the first look that an employer will get of you. Make sure that your resume is professional, well written and grammatically correct. If you fail to remember these important guidelines you might miss out on a great opportunity that you are qualified for.

# Get Your Resume to the Right People

Once your resume is polished and ready to submit, make sure that it ends up in the hands of the person doing the hiring. This will ensure that those making decisions actually see your resume instead of your resume getting lost in the shuffle.

This involves doing your research. Contact the company and ask who is responsible for hiring. In large companies there may be several people involved in the process. Try to find out who does the hiring for your specific department (accounting, human resources, etc.).

When mailing a resume make sure that you address it to the person that you want to receive it. The same is true when faxing. Consider using a cover sheet that clearly states the recipient of the fax.

If you found this opening on a job board, make sure that you follow any instructions provided in the posting carefully. If the job posting says to fax your resume to a certain number, fax it there. On the other hand, if they ask for resumes to be emailed, make sure that you do that. Employers want employees that will listen and follow directions. Neglecting instructions may disqualify you for a position that would otherwise be yours.

# The Interview

## The Interview

Once you create a polished resume that shows what you can offer a company, the calls should start coming in. Most likely you will be asked to interview. While landing an interview is an important step in the hiring process, don't assume that this means that the job is yours. It is still up to you to put your best foot forward and to impress the potential employer.

## Dress for the Occasion

Don't show up to your interview wearing faded jean shorts and a tank top. Instead use this opportunity to impress the potential employer with your professional appearance. While your clothing choice might not be the determining factor in getting the job, they can give you an advantage and encourage the interviewer to pay attention.

Men should wear suits, collared shirts in a conservative color and a tie. Avoid wearing brightly colored ties or character ties. Wear dress shoes that are freshly polished. If you plan on bringing supporting documentation, bring a briefcase or portfolio along. Men should remove earrings, necklaces and bracelets and should never wear makeup to an interview.

Women should generally wear a business suit with a skirt. Make sure that the skirt is not too short. When you sit down it should cover your thighs. They should pair this with a conservative blouse or shirt. Jewelry and makeup are appropriate and encouraged. Avoid wearing too much makeup or flashy jewelry pieces. Wear conservative and well maintained dress shoes. Generally sandals, stilettos and tennis shoes should be avoided. Women should wear nylons or tights, but not funky colors or wild patterns.

On the day of your interview make sure that everything is clean and wrinkle free. Many people are sensitive to certain scents and it is a good idea to avoid wearing perfume, cologne or heavily scented lotions. Facial piercings should be removed and tattoos should be covered. Never wear sunglasses, a cell phone earpiece or headphones into an interview. Remove these and put them away before entering the building.

To avoid unexpected interruptions always turn off your cell phone and make sure that the timer on your watch won't be going off during the interview.

# What Do You Need to Bring to an Interview?

Always bring along a couple extra copies of your resume to your interview. This way you are prepared with another copy if the interviewer does not have a copy of your resume. It is also a good idea to bring along your professional portfolio if you have one and any documentation that may be requested during the interview. Have a pen and paper handy in case you need to make any notes or fill out any forms while waiting. Bring these documents and paperwork in a briefcase or portfolio case. Never carry them by hand and never bring them in a backpack.

Bring a list of references and a list of questions for the employer. It is likely that they will ask if you have any questions and it is a good idea to be prepared. Employment documentation like proof of education, your driver's license and social security card might also be needed.

Also bring along a little cash. In some cases you will need to park in a paid parking lot or next to a parking meter. Having cash will make parking a lot easier and will reduce your stress if you do end up having to pay for parking.

# Preparing for Tough Questions

During your interview some tough questions will come up. If you were fired from your last job or if you are unemployed it is important to prepare your answers in advance so that you are ready with a positive response to these difficult questions. Knowing how to answer questions about being firing can make the difference in impressing the employer and getting the job or missing out on an opportunity.

# Figure Out What Went Wrong

The first step in being able to explain your unemployment or firing is to determine what went wrong. It is possible that you were fired for no fault of your own. Perhaps there were personality conflicts between you and a supervisor or maybe the company decided to go in another direction. It is also possible that you made mistakes that led to you losing your job. Figure out why you were fired and what lessons you learned from this experience.

# Practice Interview Questions and Answers

It is a good idea to create a list of potential interview questions and answers so that you will be prepared with quality answers when asked. Create a list of potential interview questions and practice positive and enthusiastic answers to these questions. Remember when interviewing that it is important to tell the truth. The trick is learning to use the truth to make a negative into a positive in the employer's eyes.

# Why Were You Fired?

There are several ways to answer the question, "Why were you fired?" The key to nailing this difficult question is preparation and a well thought out answer. Here are a few ideas to try:

Explain that you made mistakes but have learned from them. It might also be helpful to explain how this knowledge will benefit the employer. "I made some mistakes on a large project which unfortunately led to my termination. Through this experience I learned the importance of prioritizing responsibilities and relying on my team. I would love to put these skills to use in your company."

If the firing wasn't your fault, be sure to let the employer know. Say something like, "My company was really hit by the recession and had to downsize most of their staff. My position was one of the jobs that were eliminated. I am excited to put my skills to use for your company."

If you were fired for reasons due to job performance explain how the situation is now different. "I was going through some personal struggles that got in the way of my being able to perform my job in the manner expected. I have resolved these issues and am ready to become a valuable member of a team once again."

Sometimes personality conflict can result in a termination. If this is the case make sure that your interviewer knows that you generally work well with others. "I take pride in my ability to get along well with a variety of different personalities. In this situation my supervisor and I didn't see eye to eye. I don't know what the problem was but I don't expect this to ever happen again. I am a team player and enjoy working with under many different leadership styles."

Always be positive and always end your answers by explaining the benefit that you are ready to provide to the company. Employers want to know what problems you can solve for their company and if you explain how your bad experience can benefit them, they will listen.

## What Have You Been Doing During the 6 Months You Have Been Unemployed?

If you have a long period of unemployment on your resume, you will likely be asked about it during the interview. Here are some strategies to use when answering this question.

If the period of unemployment on your resume is due to a position that you chose not to include now is the perfect time to explain it. Say something like, "During that time I took on a position working as an account specialist. I quickly realized that it wasn't a good fit for my skill set and didn't include it on my resume since the skills utilized there did not apply to this position. This position is a better fit for my skills and abilities."

If you have been doing consulting or freelance work make sure that you mention this when responding to this question. You might say, "During the time that I have been searching for work I have been supporting my family by running a small consulting business. This has helped me to hone my organizational skills and has taught me the importance of clear communication with clients. I am ready to head back into the work place and put these skills to use for your company."

Training and education can also make a good explanation for times of unemployment. "When I was laid off from my last position I realized that it was important to go back to school and get an education. During this time I received a certificate in bookkeeping and had the chance to learn some of the industry's latest software programs.

# Why Wouldn't You be an Ideal Candidate for this Position?

This question is a tricky one. You must answer it, but do not want to give the employer any reason not to hire you. Consider saying something like, "I applied for this position because I believe that I am a good match for what you are looking for. However I do tend to put my best effort into every position that I hold. If you are looking for someone to do the bare minimum, then I am not a good candidate for this job since I always go above and beyond what is expected."

As you can see this response takes a negative question and finds a positive answer. Of course every employer will want an employee willing to give additional effort to their company.

# Tell Me About Yourself

This difficult question isn't a question at all, but is generally one the candidates struggle with the most. As you answer this question remember to keep everything directed to the position that you are applying for. Here are some tips to keep in mind.

This is the perfect opportunity to sell yourself to your employer. Say something like, "I was recently laid off after working for my past employer for almost 10 years. I learned a lot while working there and am ready to put my skills to use in a new position."

You can even use your hobbies and interests to sell yourself. "I am an avid computer programmer. When I am not working I love creating computer programs and applications for family and friends. I believe that my strong programming skills make me an ideal match for your programming position. Since programming is a passion as well as a skill. I enjoy what I do and this enthusiasm translates to my projects."

# Do You Have Any Questions for Me?

This question is often one of the last questions asked during an interview. This question might seem optional, but it is not. If you want to really impress, this is your opportunity. Create a list of well thought out questions. Not only will you learn a little more about the company but you will also show your critical thinking skills and further express your interest in the position.

Ask about the company. You could try asking a question like, "How does the company plan to move forward in spite of the difficult economic conditions?" or, "What are the biggest challenges facing the company at this time?" This question is best asked when you are interviewing with company executives or those involved in day to day company operations.

Ask about the work environment. Questions like, "What is the work environment like? I find that I work best under pressure when I have specific and measurable objectives to meet each day."

Asking questions that show your desire to stay with the company long term can be a good idea. You might want to say something like, "What types of training and professional development does the company offer? I am looking for a position that will allow me to remain with the company for a long time while honing my skills."

Consider asking when the final decision is expected. "When do you expect to make your final decision about who to hire for this position?"

Keep your questions to a minimum. In general it is a good idea to have a few questions prepared, by try to keep your list five questions or less. It isn't a good idea to ask about salary or benefits.

Don't ask questions that make you seem unreliable or unprofessional. For example questions like, "What is the company policy on sick days?" or, "I like to have a drink or two at lunch to calm my nerves. Is that acceptable?" should be avoided.

## After the Interview

Once the interview has ended gather your belongings and exit the building. It is not a good idea to hang around. If you are interviewing in a retail or restaurant environment, do not stop to shop or eat after the interview. This appears unprofessional. You can return at a later time for these activities.

Always send a thank you to your interviewer after the meeting. Try to send it as soon as possible. This doesn't necessarily need to be mailed. If you like you can also send an email thank you. Remember that once the interview process is started the hiring decision will follow very shortly. Quick response is needed if you want to make an impact before the hiring is completed.

In your thank you simply thank the interviewer for their time, reaffirm your interest in the position and remind the interviewer of your qualifications. It should be short and to the point. Many people realize that they have forgotten important information during the interview. If this is the case your thank you letter is a great time to add this information in. Always proof read carefully before sending.

# Good Luck!

Getting a new job after getting fired might not be a walk in the park, but it is possible. Losing your job isn't the end of the world and it might end up being a great opportunity for you. Once you have had several successful interviews the job offers should start rolling in. Choose a great job, put your best foot forward and impress your new employer.

Remember that even the best planned and executed job hunt can take time. Don't get discouraged. Spend time hunting for jobs each day and you will find a great new opportunity in no time at all. Getting fired doesn't diminish who you are or what you can provide to employers.

# Resources

http://jobsearch.about.com/od/unemployment/a/fileunemploy.htm

http://mtgprofessor.com/A%20-%20Payment%20Problems/what_should_you_do_when_you_can%27t_pay.htm

http://jobsearch.about.com/od/salary/a/fired.htm

http://www.free-resume-tips.com/10tips.html

http://www.quintcareers.com/dressing_at_the_interview.html

http://www.ctdol.state.ct.us/youth/interviewing-bring.htm

http://www.job-interview-site.com/do-you-have-any-questions-for-me-interview-question-and-answers.html

http://www.bbb.org/us/article/5392

# About Minute Help Press

Minute Help Press is building a library of books for people with only minutes to spare. Follow @minutehelp on Twitter to receive the latest information about free and paid publications from Minute Help Press, or visit minutehelpguides.com.

www.ingramcontent.com/pod-product-compliance
Lightning Source LLC
Chambersburg PA
CBHW051243170526
45165CB00004B/1556